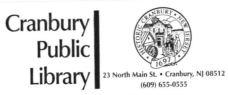

What Can Swim?

Patricia Whitehouse

Heinemann Library
Chicago, Illinois

© 2004 Heinemann Library
a division of Reed Elsevier Inc.
Chicago, Illinois

Customer Service 888-454-2279
Visit our website at www.heinemannlibrary.com

Designed by Sue Emerson, Heinemann Library; Page layout by Que-Net Media™
Printed and bound in the U.S.A. by Lake Book Manufacturing
Photo research by Bill Broyles

08 07 06 05 04
10 9 8 7 6 5 4 3 2 1

Library of Congress Cataloging-in-Publication Data
Whitehouse, Patricia, 1958-
  What can swim? / Patricia Whitehouse.
       v. cm. – (What can?)
Contents: What is swimming? – How do living things swim? – Can birds swim? – Can creatures without legs swim? – Can big animals swim? – Can animals with flippers swim? – Can bugs swim? – Can machines swim? – Can people swim?
  ISBN 1-4034-4368-8 (HC), 1-4034-4375-0 (Pbk.)
  1. Swimming–Juvenile literature. 2. Animal swimming–Juvenile literature. [1. Swimming. 2. Animal swimming.]
I. Title.
  QP310.S95W48 2003
  573.7'9–dc21

                                   2003001009

Acknowledgments
The author and publishers are grateful to the following for permission to reproduce copyright material:
p. 4 M. C. Chamberlain/DRK Photo; p. 5T Stephen J. Krasemann/DRK Photo; p. 5B Doug Perrine/DRK Photo; p. 6 Tony Arruza/Corbis; p. 7T Marty Snyderman/Visuals Unlimited; p. 7B Norbert Wu/DRK Photo; p. 8 Jane Burton/Bruce Coleman Inc.; p. 9 Raymond Coleman/Visuals Unlimited; p. 10 Edward Lines/John G. Shedd Aquarium/Visuals Unlimited; p. 11 Joel Arrington/Visuals Unlimited; p. 12 Phillip Colla/Seapics.com; p. 13 W. Perry Conway/Corbis; p. 14 E. & P. Buer/ Bruce Coleman Inc.; p. 15 Tom Brakefield/DRK Photo; p. 16 William Leonard/DRK Photo; p. 17 Gary Meszaros/Visuals Unlimited; p. 18 Lockheed Martin; p. 19 M. Timothy O'Keefe/Bruce Coleman Inc.; p. 20 George Shelley/Corbis; p. 21 Pete Saloutos/Corbis; p. 22 (row 1, L-R) Corbis, Corbis, S. Maslowski/Visuals Unlimited; (row 2, L-R) Peggy Heard/Frank Lane Picture Agency/Corbis, Kim Saar/Heinemann Library; p. 23 (row 1, L-R) Marty Snyderman/ Visuals Unlimited, Charles O'Rear/Corbis, Pete Saloutos/Corbis; (row 2, L-R) Tom Brakefield/DRK Photo, Edward Lines/John G. Shedd Aquarium/ Visuals Unlimited, S. Maslowski/Visuals Unlimited; (row 3) M. Timothy O'Keefe/Bruce Coleman Inc.; p. 24 (row 1, L-R) W. Perry Conway/Corbis, S. Maslowski/Visuals Unlimited, Pete Saloutos/Corbis; (row 2, L-R) Peggy Heard/Frank Lane Picture Agency/Corbis, Kim Saar/Heinemann Library; back cover (L-R) M. C. Chamberlain/DRK Photo, Joel Arrington/Visuals Unlimited

Cover photograph by W. Perry Conway/Corbis

Special thanks to our advisory panel for their help in the preparation of this book:

Alice Bethke, Library Consultant
Palo Alto, CA

Eileen Day, Preschool Teacher
Chicago, IL

Kathleen Gilbert,
Second Grade Teacher
Round Rock, TX

Sandra Gilbert,
Library Media Specialist
Fiest Elementary School
Houston, TX

Jan Gobeille,
Kindergarten Teacher
Garfield Elementary
Oakland, CA

Angela Leeper,
Educational Consultant
Wake Forest, NC

Some words are shown in bold, **like this.**
You can find them in the picture glossary on page 23.

Contents

What Is Swimming?

Swimming is a way of moving.

Things that swim move through water.

Some things only use part of their bodies to swim.

Other things use their whole bodies to swim.

How Do Living Things Swim?

Some living things use their legs or feet to swim.

This dog uses its front and back legs to swim.

fin

flipper

Some living things use special
body parts.

Fins, flippers, or **webbed feet**
help animals swim.

Can Birds Swim?

webbed feet

Birds with **webbed feet** can swim.

Ducks have webbed feet and can swim.

A dove is a bird that cannot swim.

It does not have webbed feet.

Can Creatures without Legs Swim?

fin

Seahorses are a kind of fish.

They have one **fin** that moves when they swim.

Snakes do not have legs.

Some snakes can swim by wiggling their bodies through the water.

Can Big Animals Swim?

Whales are heavy and can swim.

Blue whales are the biggest animals on Earth!

Polar bears are big, heavy animals that swim in cold water.

They move their legs to swim.

Can Animals with Flippers Swim?

flipper

Walruses have four **flippers** instead of legs.

The two back flippers push this walrus through the water.

flipper

Penguins have two flippers instead of wings.

Penguins move their flippers to swim underwater.

Can Bugs Swim?

Mosquitoes come out of eggs in the water.

They can only swim when they are young.

Giant water bugs are good swimmers.

They catch tadpoles, fish, and other bugs to eat.

Can Machines Swim?

Some machines can move underwater, like this **robot**.

But machines cannot swim.

propeller

This submarine moves underwater.

It has **propellers** that move it.

Can People Swim?

People can swim.

They move their arms and legs
in the water.

swim fins

Some people use special tools to help them swim.

These **swim fins** help the girl swim faster.

Quiz

Which of these things can swim?

Can you find them in the book?

Picture Glossary

fin
pages 7, 10

robot
page 18

swim fins
page 21

flipper
pages 7, 14, 15

seahorse
page 10

webbed feet
pages 7, 8, 9

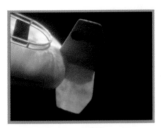
propellers
page 19

Note to Parents and Teachers

Reading for information is an important part of a child's literacy development. Learning begins with a question about something. Help children think of themselves as investigators and researchers by encouraging their questions about the world around them. Each chapter in this book begins with a question that helps categorize the types of things that swim. Read each question together. Look at the pictures. Can children think of other swimming things in each category? Discuss where you might find the answers. Assist children in using the picture glossary and the index to practice new vocabulary and research skills.

Index

Answers to quiz on page 22

Polar bears, ducks, and people can swim.

Doves and cars cannot swim.